Cardiff Libraries
www.cardiff.gov.uk/libraries
Llyfrgelloedd Caerdyd
D0305458

Quarter Life Poetry
Poems for the young, broke & hangry
SAMANTHA JAYNE

sphere

SPHERE

First published in the US by Grand Central Publishing in 2016
First published in Great Britain in 2016 by Sphere

1 3 5 7 9 10 8 6 4 2

A CIP catalogue record for this book
is available from the British Library.

ISBN 978-0-7515-6667-3

Printed in China

Sphere
An imprint of
Little, Brown Book Group
Carmelite House
50 Victoria Embankment
London EC4Y 0DZ

An Hachette UK Company
www.hachette.co.uk

www.littlebrown.co.uk

To my parents,
for putting up with my bullshit

Introduction

I've been told this is a good bathroom book. I have mixed feelings. Mostly because I didn't envision my first published work to sit atop toilets—let alone *my* toilet in a tiny, sad bathroom fit for a homeless elf. I thought things would look different by twenty-five—that I'd reap the rewards of my hard work and excellent life choices. I'd have timeless wardrobe pieces, premium cable, an inspired sex life, and a goddamn human-sized spa-bathroom complete with a gentle bidet and waterfall shower. Instead, I have student loans and Thai leftovers I'm mildly excited about.

But perhaps you have a tiny bathroom, too. Maybe things aren't quite how you expected them to be. So you know what? Display this book on your toilet. Maybe some of these poems will even make you laugh. Which makes me laugh, because now you're laughing alone in your bathroom. But maybe, at this exact moment, someone else is sitting on their toilet, reading the same poem, and laughing alone, too. And I suppose that's the whole point of this book—that you're not alone at all. And sometimes all we need is to laugh together from our separate toilets.

Struggles

Routine

My friend has a baby
and owns a boutique.
I just bought a cactus;
it died in a week.

Someday I'll own a chic abode
embellished with fine art.
Till then I'll deal with walls so thin
I hear my roommate fart.

I've been so busy
I hadn't a chance
to shave my two legs—
now my hair looks like pants.

I thought living the grown-up life
would be so freakin' sweet.
Instead I work and trudge on home
to pass out, rinse, repeat.

I'm longing for the special day
of signing my own lease,
so clothing can be optional
and I can poop in peace.

In case of a catastrophe,
I've made myself a kit.
It's essential for survival–
so far there's wine in it.

The bedroom listing
said “a room with a view.”
I just wish I knew
that the view was the loo.

I nearly collapsed
when I heard myself say,
"I don't understand
the youth of today."

Forget the fancy gym contract
with fine print no one reads.
My fifth-floor walk-up apartment
is all that my ass needs.

There's a wrinkle on my forehead
and a pimple on my nose.
It's difficult to illustrate
my despair in prose.

I used to wax my lady bits,
but recently I've quit.
I had this grand epiphany
that I don't give a shit.

If I stretch out my arms
and my legs really wide,
I can measure the box
that I'm living inside.

A tragic part of postgrad life
is no student ID.
It was my golden ticket
to getting shit for free.

Today I saw a baby
with such cuteness and grace,
I thought, “aw, I want a baby,”
but then I punched myself in the face.

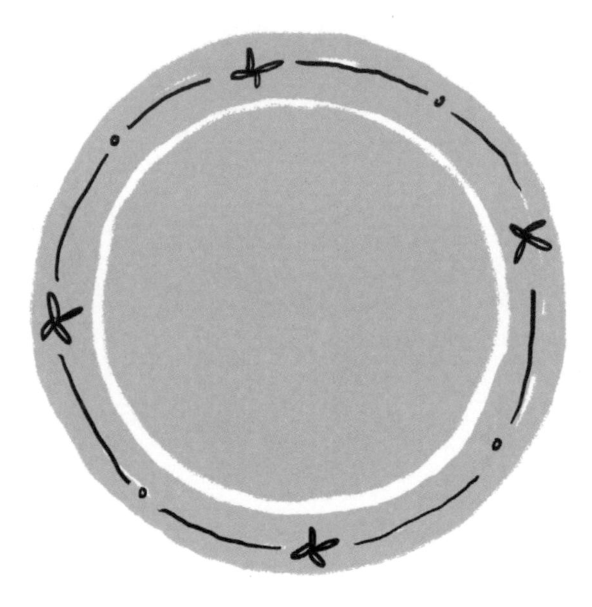

Someday I'll lead a lavish life
where I own many lands,
and I will have a dishwasher
that won't be my two hands.

They say in your twenties
each moment is priceless
if each moment isn't
an existential crisis.

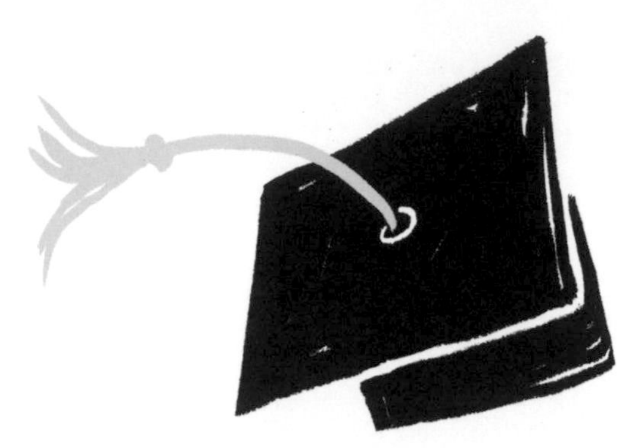

Now that I've earned my degree
and made summa cum laude,
it's time I rethink my whole life
and run away abroad.

I had a dream the other night
of strange, mystical lands
with flying bunnies, unicorns,
and 401(k) plans.

I can't afford a Zen garden
or tranquility pond,
so I'll unwind by wandering
through Bed Bath & Beyond.

The other day I calculated
costs to buy a home,
and I deduced I can afford
a nice big garden gnome.

On Fridays when I get paid
I go hard like a baller—
that is, until my rent is due
and I return to squalor.

I don't need to exercise
'cause I already sweat
when I contemplate the depth
of my student loan debt.

My alma mater implored me
to send them a donation.
If anything, I should write them
an equal invitation.

Now that I'm mature enough,
I'm asking the big questions,
like how much can I really get
for my Beanie Baby collection?

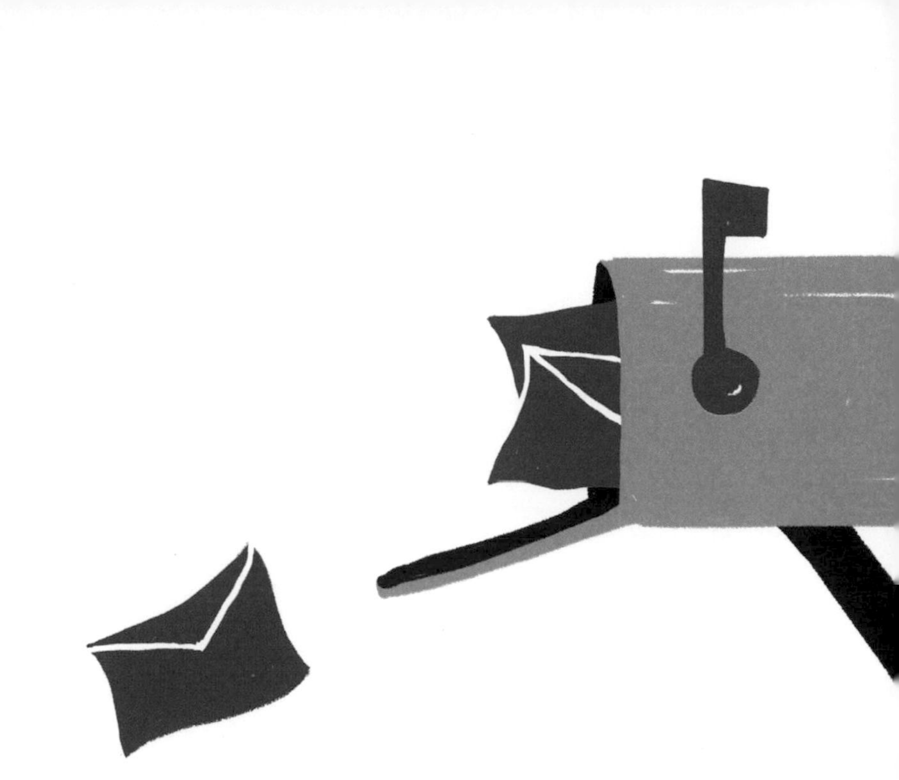

I can do anything
I put my mind to
except pay my bills
at the time they are due.

My five-year plan
has been going great,
ever since I postponed it
for another eight.

My degree was paramount
to expanding possibilities
of things I'd do to pay off loans
and quadruple my humility.

I wonder if this month,
instead of money,
my landlord would accept
a bundt cake with honey.

Credit cards have faith in me;
I feel profoundly moved.
The deeper that I sink in debt,
the more I'm pre-approved.

A letter! For me?
Do I have pen pals still?
Or perhaps a secret admirer?
It's my insurance bill.

It's time for a dramatic change.
I'll jet set without care!
Oh, there's six dollars to my name.
I'll just cut my hair.

Someday in my future
it would be dandy
to visit the bank
for more than free candy.

I refer to myself
as my father's princess.
I remind him of this
in financial distress.

I'm fiscally responsible
and saving large amounts
when I'm streaming TV shows
from my parents' account.

Food

I'm undertaking a new skill.
For this I must be brave:
I shall attempt to cook something
without a microwave.

I am a skilled magician:
when I foresee a meal,
I hit a magic button
and it appears for real.

As a responsible adult,
I must nourish myself
with ice cream, chocolates, gummy bears
and corn chips from the shelf.

The waiting list was dismal,
the trek there was a pain,
but my muffin got twelve likes,
so brunch was not in vain.

I ordered Thai delivery;
didn't feel like walking there.
I'd have to put on a bra,
and they know I live upstairs.

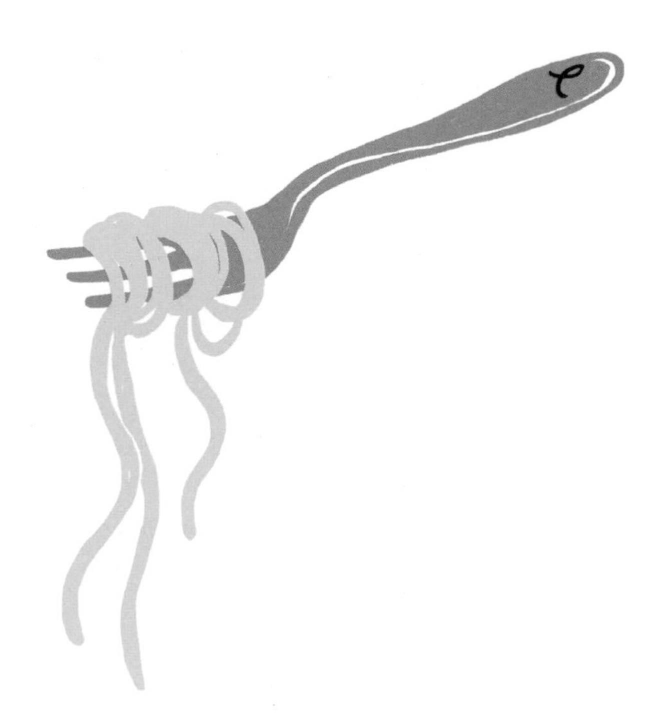

Summer is coming!
I'll help you get ready
by eating your half-finished
plate of spaghetti.

Is it a late-night booty call
when the request is "Please,
can somebody deliver
a large plain pie with cheese?"

My general productivity
and brilliant thoughts I think
positively correlate
with the caffeine I drink.

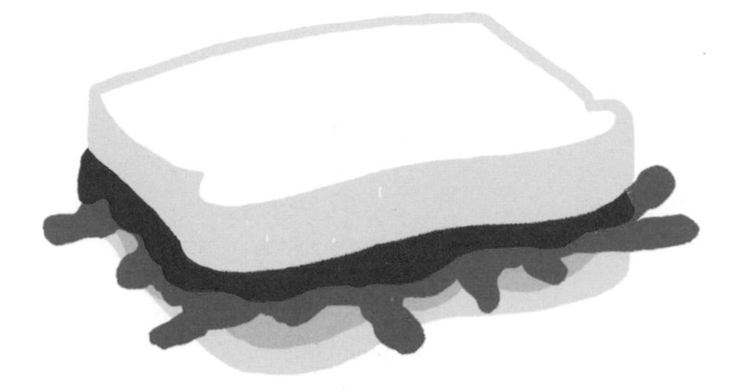

Peanut butter and jelly
is a world class dinner,
but stuff it up with Cheetos–
it's a culinary winner.

I'm on a juice cleanse,
and it's going fine.
The juice is fermented–
okay…it's just wine.

I hate everyone
I pass in the street.
It's mostly because
I forgot to eat.

I'm on a strict new diet,
and how it works is great:
the calories don't count at all
if I eat them from your plate.

This bump in my belly
will not need a crib;
for it's not a baby,
but baby back ribs.

Sorry, women's magazines.
I'll need a better reason
to refuse delicious food
than 'cause it's swimsuit season.

When I'm asked of future plans
that I may have in sight,
I describe in great detail
what I will eat tonight.

I should be a beacon,
a shining example,
not crouched at the cheese shop
inhaling free samples.

My breakfast was a Pop-Tart.
I ate some grapes at noon.
What shall I cook for dinner?
Hummus on a spoon.

A simple life lesson
to avoid getting hurt:
Never trust someone
who dislikes dessert.

Let us all gather ’round
as we mourn side by side
to commemorate the fateful day
my metabolism died.

Social Life

When no one carded me tonight
I felt deeply offended.
I poured my wine onto the floor,
for my youth has ended.

When weighing evening options
of social life or bed,
I'll go out if it's guaranteed
at some point I'll be fed.

Girls night's a time
of tapas and wine
and fierce validation
that we'll all be fine.

I'm certain that my friends and I
have bloomed into grown-ups
because we drink at house parties
without red plastic cups.

With one-fourth of my life lived
I can't waste any time.
I must resolve how to bypass
the women's bathroom line.

When I go out for power lunch
with friends who have careers,
I spend more on one side dish
than I would make in years.

Let's avoid the bars tonight.
I wish to not impose
on the mating rituals
of local college bros.

I often reflect that my life
is not going as planned.
It's mostly when I'm forced to watch
my roommate's boyfriend's band.

My roommate stole my yogurt
out of the kitchen fridge,
so I set fire to her clothes
and threw them off a bridge.

My friends are dancing at the club,
but I've got plans instead
to have a crazy, wild night
baking banana bread.

I saw my favorite band tonight,
but that's not the best part:
instead of standing on my feet
there was a seating chart.

As my friends voyage
to lands wide and far,
I watch free cable
at the neighborhood bar.

No, you should go out.
I'm perfectly fine
with drowning my sorrows
in two-dollar wine.

So sad I can't make it
to bottomless brunch.
I'm bottomless in bed
with Cinnamon Toast Crunch.

11:50 Friday night.
The bars are filling up.
Me, I'm naked on the couch
with ramen in a cup.

In my early twenties
gossip made me stressed,
but lately I don't give a shit
'cause I'm the fucking best.

I used to guzzle all the booze
and wake up perky-eyed,
but lately mornings after drinks
I feel like I have died.

Sex

He texted "what u wearing ;)?"
I gave myself a glance:
"a cat-themed XL sweatshirt
and some wine-stained stretchy pants."

I don't believe in labels
when referring to my man,
mostly because "fuck buddy"
was not what I had planned.

I used to bolt from one-night stands
so I would not intrude,
but nowadays I stick around
until they buy me food.

This one-night stand turned second date
is an uncommon case.
It's honestly because I left
my charger at his place.

Dressing up for a night out
drowns me in dread and gloom.
If I just sext with my ex
I needn't leave my room.

I went out on a solo date
to the best froyo chain,
then I invited myself home
and the sex was insane.

I cannot say I have regrets
for my many a tryst.
I write them down and call myself
a gonzo journalist.

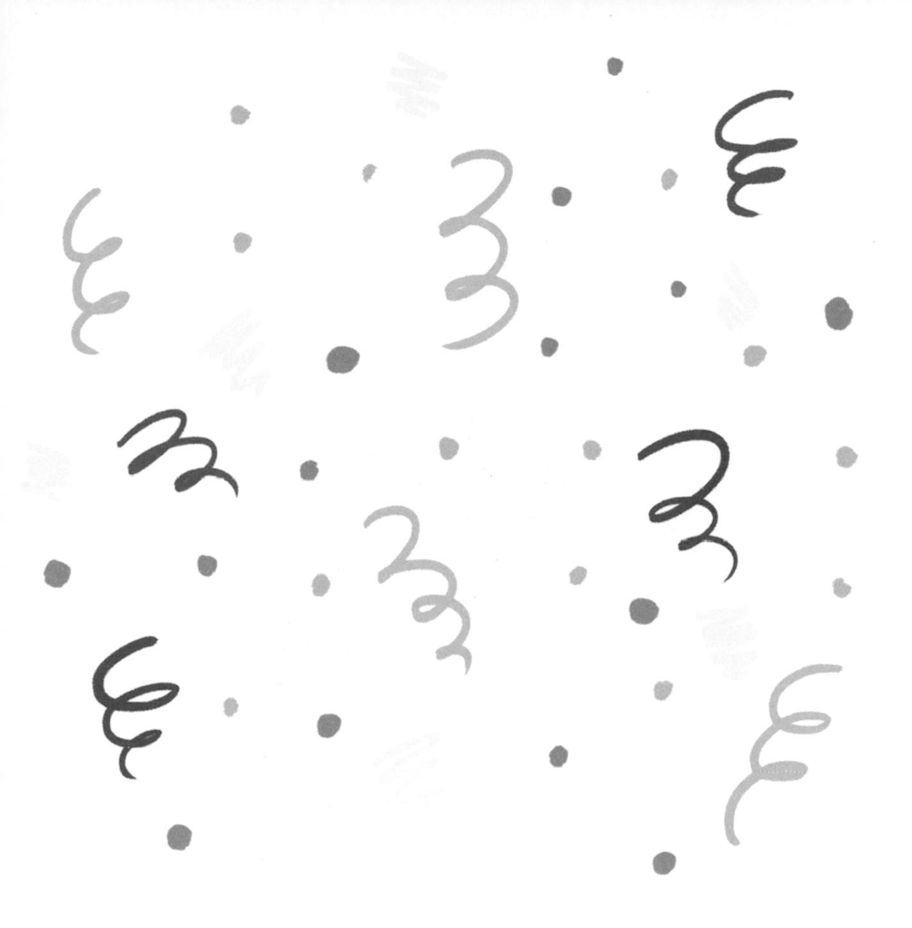

Some call it a walk of shame,
but it's a celebration!
I'm proclaiming my release
of sexual frustration.

I had a foursome
two nights ago
with Ben and Jerry
and HBO GO.

Some say the best sex
is when you're in love.
For me, it's my neighbor
I forget the name of.

This Valentine's Day
I had plans for a winner:
I dressed up my dildo
and took it to dinner.

I have a friend with benefits;
he's really quite a catch.
Those benefits are health and dental
with a 401(k) match.

I'm well versed as a single chick
on positions in the sack.
My specialties are fetal and
sprawled out wide on my back.

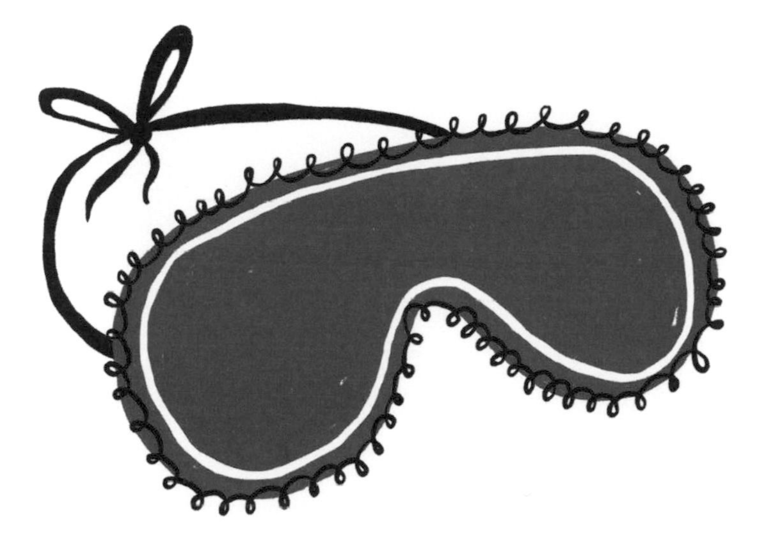

He leaned in close and beckoned me
to divulge my deepest fantasy.
I sighed and whispered lustfully,
"to pay off my postgrad degree."

I think I might be pregnant.
There's a burning in my heart;
I'm bloated, cramped, and achy.
Oh—I just had to fart.

According to the laws
of California State,
my vibrator is officially
my legal domestic mate.

He bragged he's a "musician"
to which I was annoyed.
I'm old enough to understand
that's code for unemployed.

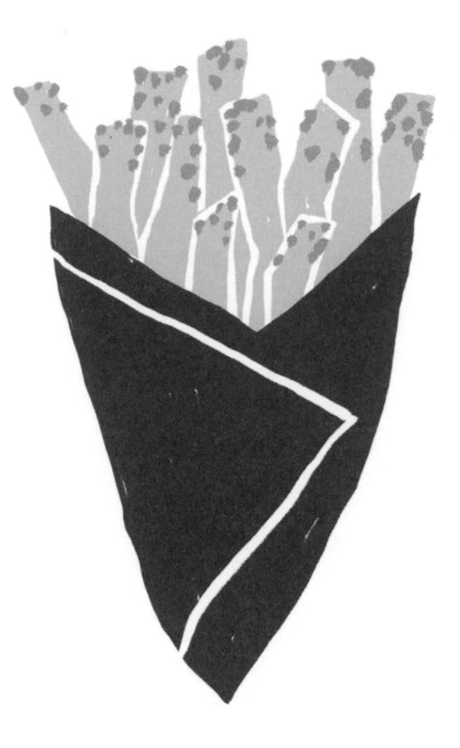

The last time
I felt butterflies
was when I ordered
truffle fries.

Browsing my feed,
I'm delighted to see
your new girlfriend is
the ugly version of me.

If I had a boyfriend,
I'd make our courtship count.
We'd add up to the minimum
delivery amount.

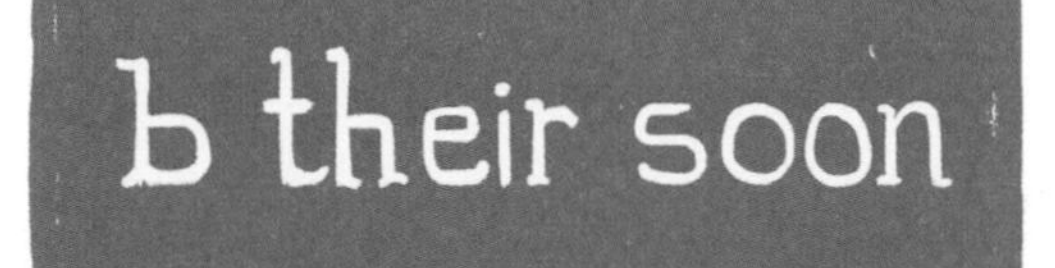

I don't need to be showered
in chocolates and fine wine.
A text with proper grammar
would do me just fine.

First dates make me a nervous wreck.
Can we just skip ahead
to burping loudly as we binge
on *Game of Thrones* in bed?

Yesterday my true love died;
he lost his rosy glow.
Truth is I hadn't watered him
since three full weeks ago.

I'm trying hard in dating life
to not be such a snob.
He needn't have a great career,
just any fucking job.

I stand as a proud feminist
in all I do and say–
but if I'm dined on a first date,
he better fucking pay.

Tickety-tock
goes my clock–
my mother says
each time we talk.

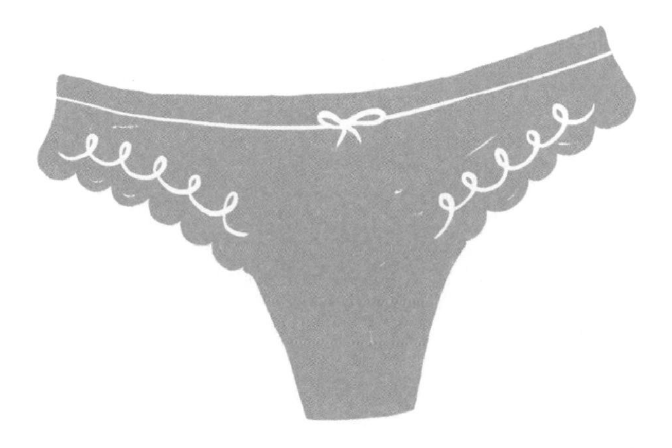

I love being single!
There's no one to care
if I spend two days
in the same underwear.

My mother's brimming with advice
she carefully compiled,
mostly regarding how to raise
my hypothetical child.

In my dear grandmother's eyes
my situation's dire:
I must find a virile mate
before my eggs expire.

When I had a crush,
I used to be shy.
Now I lick my lips
and stare him in the eye.

Perhaps I'll tell my future kids
of the fateful night
"when Mom and Dad fell in love,
we first both swiped right."

I have a chilling tale
of a nightmare come to life:
I slipped and double-tapped a pic
of my ex-boyfriend's wife.

Weddings

I can no longer find my fridge.
All I'm able to see
is a structure that displays
a wedding invite gallery.

My friend's wedding invite
includes a plus-one.
Oh, that's such a relief
'cause my cat is so fun.

The next wedding I attend
I have resolved to bring
a plastic bag to sneak home snacks,
and I'll feast like a king.

I'm delighted for my Facebook friends
who are blushing brides-to-be,
but one more staged proposal pic
and you're all dead to me.

I have a small bed
but can't afford bedding.
I went broke on a gift
for my roommate's friend's wedding.

As every girl I ever knew
exclaims "yes to the dress,"
I'm content in my status:
"perpetual hot mess."

My friend's wedding day,
I caught the bouquet,
and then I made out
with the drunk DJ.

Fashion

It's fun to buy a fancy dress
off the designer's rack
to wear it once and keep the tags
to get my money back.

My pants are too tight
and my shirt shrunk up higher.
What could be the culprit:
dessert or the dryer?

My wardrobe is a frightful mess
of blunders I once wore,
stained old sweats, and T-shirts from
my dear boyfriends of yore.

There's no freedom I could feel
that matches the degree
of unhinging my bra at night
and setting my boobs free.

Vintage is “in.”
I call that a win
’cause I can afford
the donation bin.

My sweatpants lying on the rug
are definitely clean.
The crotch smells fine, and besides—
the wine stain can't be seen.

My glitter crop top
looks fucking fantastic.
I've not aged a day
out of its demographic.

I never thought that I would reach
a more sobering junction:
I can no longer purchase bras
for style over function.

Why waste money on new trends
when I can just revive
that peasant top and denim skirt
I wore once in ’05.

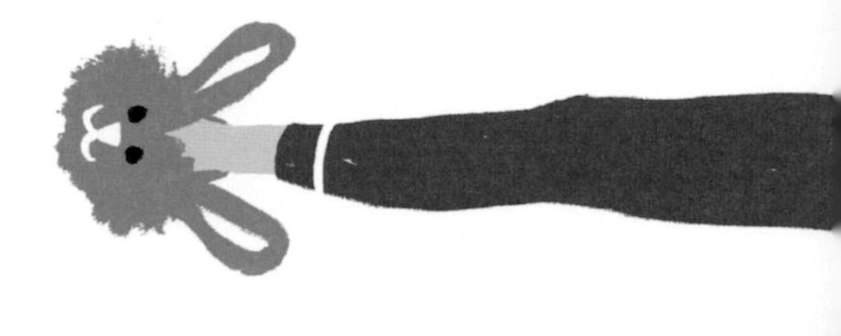

When I'm lounging around
I feel less pathetic
if I wear yoga pants–
at least I look athletic.

The tag instructs to gently rinse
then air-dry in the breeze.
Yeah, I'll just toss it in the heap
and wash it how I please.

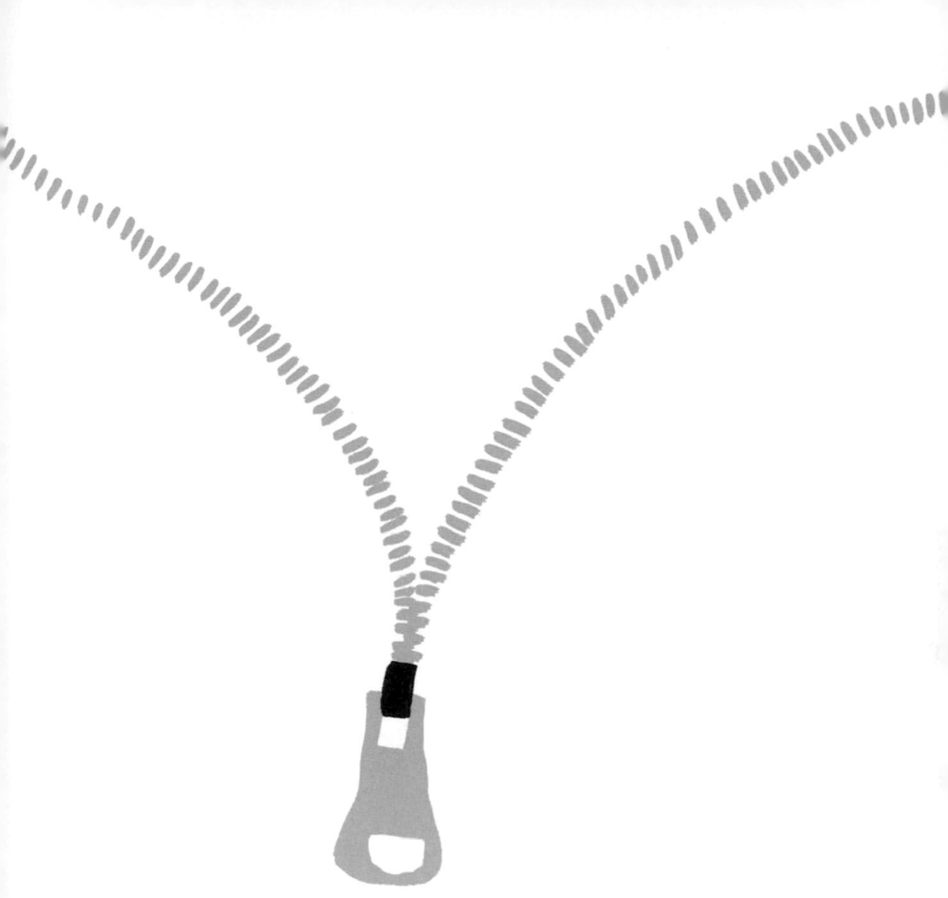

Each morning I express myself
through ultramodern dance.
It's a routine that I made up
to squeeze into my pants.

After a long winter
I unearth my bikini
then roll my eyes and heave a sigh
and throw back a martini.

My mom sent me a bizarre gift:
a medieval device—
apparently it gets real hot
and makes my clothes look nice.

Before I can love anyone
I must love myself first,
which is why I bought myself
a two-hundred-dollar purse.

Unemployment

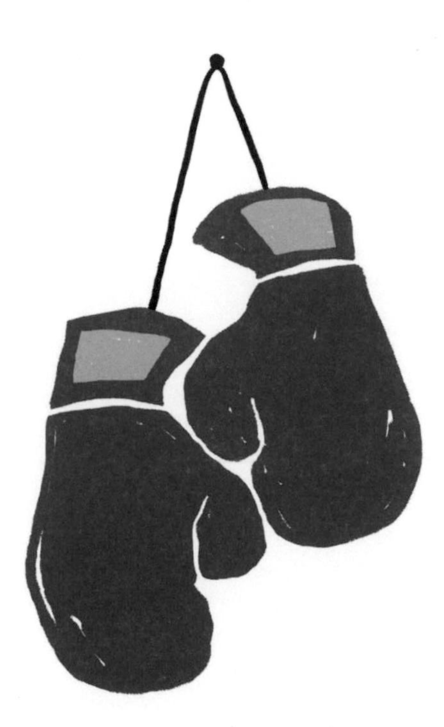

I had six rounds of interviews
and charmed 'em till I bled.
The boss's niece wanted the job,
so she's hired instead.

The '08 recession
was no Great Depression,
though I'm greatly depressed
I can't find a profession.

Working for free
would be such a treat
if I wasn't required
to pay rent or eat.

I chant mystic ancient hexes
while I shake a feathered pole
then thrust my application
into the LinkedIn black hole.

For this hostess position
I'm in stiff competition
with a Yale MBA
and a pediatrician.

My joblessness
is just life reversed!
I flip-flopped the steps
and retired first.

My application was superb,
one gem after another,
but upon listing references
I just wrote "my mother."

Socioeconomics
was a subject I enjoyed.
It gave me tools to rationalize
why I'm unemployed.

On my resume I boast
my many accolades—
namely, my attendance badge
from sixth and seventh grades.

The interviewer asked,
"What are your interests?"
I directed him to
my luxurious Pinterest.

May I revise the statement
that I gave in first grade
of what career I'd like someday
to "any job that's paid"?

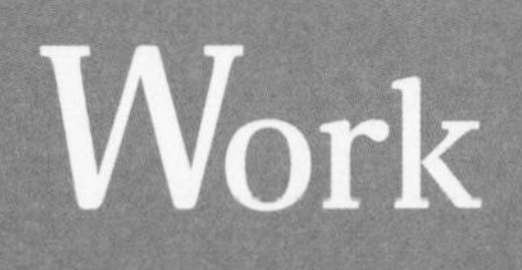
Work

I have a new job!
Well, here are the facts:
it's unpaid "experience"
but I get free snacks.

When I stare at my screen
I become introspective
and daydream of joining
a farming collective.

Your almond mocha frappe
will be $5.94.
My Master of Fine Arts
weeps silently in the drawer.

Meeting folks on my first day,
I mournfully acknowledged
my manager's the stoner kid
who I tutored in college.

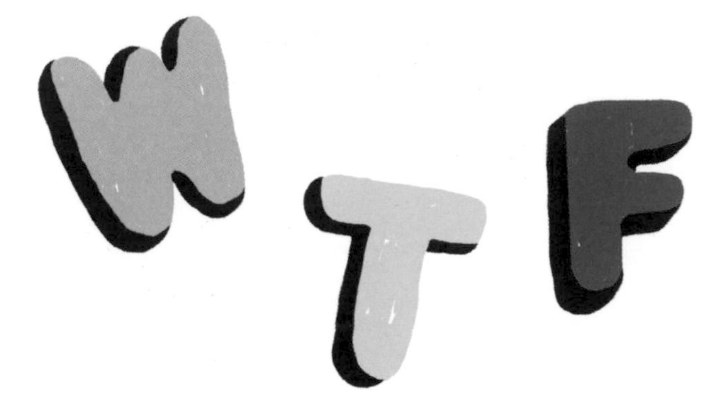

I should have listed "kindergarten"
on my resume,
'cause alphabetizing files
wasn't in my MBA.

This paycheck's amazing!
I'm making mad stacks.
Wait—where'd it all go?
Goddamn state tax.

The office perks are marvelous:
massages, drinks, events!
The only perk that's missing here
is affording my rent.

I'm a go-getter.
I wake up at dawn
and race to the office
before donuts are gone.

Without a visual barrier
between me and Creepy Chuck,
this open-office floor plan
is uncomfortable as fuck.

My boss invited me to chat.
I was brimming with joy
until he sat me down to say
he likes his lattes soy.

Dynamics in the workplace
are shockingly symbolic
of banal high school drama
but with way more alcoholics.

In a brazen blaze of glory
I'll quit and run away!
On second thought, I just recalled
tomorrow's pizza day.

Holiday parties
can be such great fun
if you crave a charade
of shitfaced everyone.

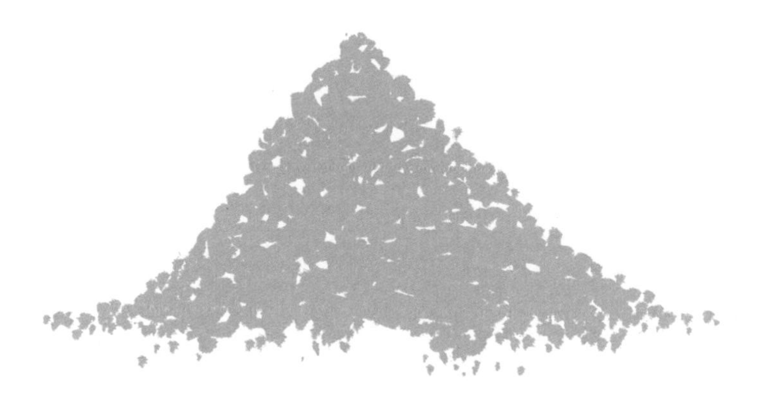

If I sit still in this cubicle
and forget to readjust,
I fear I'll slowly wither to
a pile of corporate dust.

My sociology degree
has taught me some neat tricks
on charming my rude customers
when I waitress for tips.

My one-year review
induced such great fear,
I crawled under my desk
and hid out for a year.

I wish the idea
that in fifteen years
I might still work here
didn't bring me to tears.

This corporate job crushes my soul
with the weight of hopeless doom.
I'll quit someday; till then I'll raid
free bagels in the conference room.

If my goal is to do what I love,
I haven't found it yet,
because deep down what I love most
is paying off school debt.

Life after college
is a torturous trap
of full days of work
without one single nap.

About the Author

Samantha Jayne is an actress and writer living in Los Angeles. When she isn't posting poems on her popular Tumblr and Instagram, *Quarter Life Poetry*, she writes and acts in TV and film. Her work has been featured across the web, including Buzzfeed, *Huffington Post*, PopSugar, Hello Giggles, and shared by twentysomethings everywhere.